Hari's Box

Written by Juliet Clare Bell

Illustrated by Beatriz Castro

"Everything's different," said Hari, miserably.

Mum ruffled his hair.

"Different isn't always bad," said Mum. "It can mean new friends, and new adventures."

2

"Look," said Dad.
"You've made a
friend already!"

"I've **got** friends – back
in London! Why do I need
a new one?"

Hari stamped his foot.

The cat ran off …

… and Mum stumbled,
dropping everything.

3

Hari spotted something shiny.

"Wow!" he said.
"Where did you get that?"

"Isn't it lovely?" said Mum. "Nani gave it to me when I went to university. I was unsettled – but whenever I looked at it in my new room, I felt a strong connection to home and our family history."

Mum hugged Nani.

"It was extra special to me because it had been so special to Nani."

Hari looked at the box carefully. "Why was it special to you, Nani?"

"Well," said Nani, "I got it at a very significant time in my life, when I was moving home. I was a similar age to you now, although my journey back then was very different to your journey here today."

"What do you mean?" asked Hari.

Nani bent down to Hari. "We travelled for many weeks, all the way from Southern India to England. Like you, I was very sad to leave. My grandmother, **my** nani, gave me this box and put a special note in it.

I read the note every day,
many times, on the boat."

"Where is it now?"
asked Hari.

"I took the box out on deck early one morning," said Nani. "The wind was wild, and the note blew over the edge and into the sea …

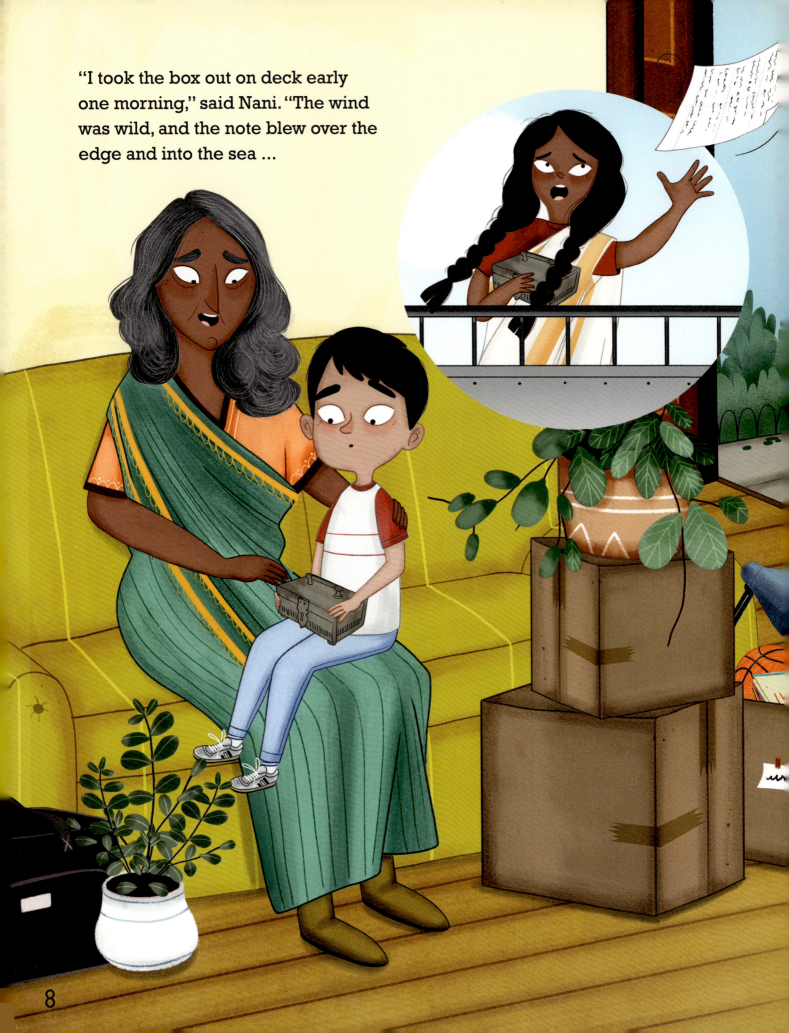

... I cried for days. But I hadn't really lost those words because they had become a part of me."

Hari pulled on Nani's hand. "What did it say?"

"She said we can only live in the present, but the wonderful things from our past remain inside of us. And for a while, in the short-term, I might feel sad about what I was leaving behind – but in the long-term, I would look back on this time as an adventure."

Dad smiled. "And it goes even further back than Nani's nani, beyond living memory. It's over 150 years old!"

"That's ancient!"

Hari stroked the box, gently. "Where did **your** nani get it from?"

"It'll be easier to show you with a picture," said Nani.

"Shall we draw a timeline on these boxes?"

Mum smiled.

"Yes, please!" said Hari.

Nani and Hari pushed some cardboard boxes together, and drew a long line across them.

"So, Mum and the shiny box are over at the end," said Nani.

"That shows when she got it from me, over twenty years ago. And I got it from **my** Nani around **here**.

Her grandfather, Nana, gave it to her to put coins in, back **here** – and **he** bought it, a very, very long time ago …"

"… all the way back **there**!" said Hari.

They looked at the timeline. It made Hari feel very small, but he also felt a bit better.

NANI

MUM

"Your box has been on a real adventure," said Hari.

"And it's not over yet." Mum looked at Nani, who nodded.
"We'd like you to have the box now."

"Really?"
whispered Hari.

"Why don't you draw yourself on
the timeline?" said Dad, dragging
over another removal box.

MUM

14

The cat ran
in again.

"Sorry!" called a girl from outside.
"She's always looking for new adventures!"

Hari smiled.

"So are we!
I'm Hari," he said.
"Would you
like to see my
new box?"

Published by Pearson Education Limited, 80 Strand, London, WC2R 0RL.

www.pearsonschools.co.uk

Text © Pearson Education Limited 2020

Written by Juliet Clare Bell

Project managed and edited by Just Content Limited

Original illustrations © Pearson Education Limited 2020

Illustrated by Beatriz Castro

Designed and typeset by Collaborate Agency Limited

First published 2020

23 22 21 20

10 9 8 7 6 5 4 3 2 1

British Library Cataloguing in Publication Data

A catalogue record for this book is available from the British Library

ISBN 978 0 435 20140 1

Printed in Slovakia by Neografia

Note from the publisher

Pearson has robust editorial processes, including answer and fact checks, to ensure the accuracy of the content in this publication, and every effort is made to ensure this publication is free of errors. We are, however, only human, and occasionally errors do occur. Pearson is not liable for any misunderstandings that arise as a result of errors in this publication, but it is our priority to ensure that the content is accurate. If you spot an error, please do contact us at resourcescorrections@pearson.com so we can make sure it is corrected.